BLS WORKING PAPERS

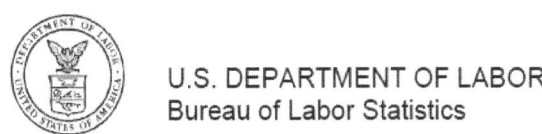

U.S. DEPARTMENT OF LABOR
Bureau of Labor Statistics

OFFICE OF EMPLOYMENT RESEARCH
AND PROGRAM DEVELOPMENT

Supervisory Status and Upper-level Supervisory Responsibilities:
Evidence from the NLSY79

Donna S. Rothstein, U.S. Bureau of Labor Statistics

Working Paper 331
September 2000

The views expressed are those of the author and do not necessarily reflect the policies of the U.S. Bureau of Labor Statistics or the views of other staff members.

Supervisory Status and Upper-level Supervisory Responsibilities:
Evidence from the NLSY79

Donna S. Rothstein, *Bureau of Labor Statistics**

Revised: August 2, 2000

*I thank Erica Groshen, Michael Horrigan, Charles Pierret, James Spletzer, Jay Stewart, and Jonathan Veum for helpful comments on an earlier version. Thanks also to Alexander Eidelman and Hector Rodriguez for excellent research assistance. The views expressed are those of the author and do not reflect the policies of the BLS or the views of other BLS staff members.

Abstract

This paper examines what it means to be a supervisor, in terms of what types of responsibilities are associated with supervisory status, who is more likely to have this authority, and what the wage consequences are from having these types of responsibilities. The results indicate that the wage returns to being a supervisor are not associated with simply having supervisory "status" or a supervisory title, per se, but rather from having associated upper-level supervisory responsibilities. While women are less likely to have supervisory status, once the status is attained, there is a small associated responsibility differential.

The attainment of supervisory status and higher-level supervisory authority represents movement up a career ladder. Significant types of responsibilities and decision-making authority can be involved with being in a supervisory role, such as setting subordinates' job tasks, evaluating their work, and having influence over their pay and promotions. Past research (mostly theoretical) has suggested that supervisors can have an important impact on worker productivity through (for example) monitoring, task allocation, and by acting in a mentoring role.[1] There is very little empirical work, however, that examines the likelihood of having supervisory responsibilities, or the effects of having these responsibilities on the worker him or herself.

This paper addresses the following questions about supervisory status and higher-level supervisory authority: who has supervisory authority and upper-level supervisory responsibilities; what are the wage consequences of having these supervisory roles. It also considers whether having supervisory status or upper-level supervisory responsibilities impacts the ability to move further up in the job hierarchy.

The empirical analysis uses a new series of questions on aspects of supervision included in the 1996 wave of the National Longitudinal Survey of Youth 1979 (NLSY79). The 1996 interview asks whether the individual is a supervisor, the types and levels of responsibilities and authority the individual has over his or her subordinates, and the number and gender of those subordinates. In 1996, the individuals in the NLSY79 ranged from ages 31 through 39. Research has shown that the early twenties are generally a period of multiple job transitions, and the thirties appear to be a time when individuals are becoming established in their career paths.[2] While the individuals in the NLSY79 may not (yet) be vying for top-most positions in their

---

[1] See, for example, Leonard (1987), Prendergast (1995), Athey, Avery, and Zemsky (forthcoming).
[2] See, for example, Gardecki and Neumark (1998).

firms, they are moving into supervisory positions, and a number have moved into positions with upper-level supervisory responsibilities.

I. The Incidence of Supervision Over Time: Evidence from the General Social Surveys

Because there is little empirical literature on supervision, as a first step I turn to a data set that shows the incidence of supervisory status among workers over time. The General Social Surveys (GSS) data set consists of a series of cross-sections from the years 1972 through 1996. In many of those years, respondents were questioned about whether they supervise anyone who is directly responsible to them. The top portion of Table 1 shows the percentage of full-time, non self-employed workers between the ages of 18 and 65 who are supervisors. The data show that a fairly high percentage of workers consider themselves to be supervisors.[3] In the 1970s, about 42% of male and 34% of female full-time workers defined themselves as supervisors. In the 1980s, this increased to about 46% for men and 40% for women, and then remained at about that level in the 1990s. It appears that for full-time workers a gender gap in supervision of about 6 to 8 percentage points has remained from the 1970s through at least the mid 1990s. This gender gap is a little bit wider (see the bottom half of Table 1), between 8 and 10 percentage points over time, when the data are restricted to individuals in their thirties—the age group that is the focus of the research in this paper.

The GSS data indicate that a large percentage of workers consider themselves to be supervisors. However, there may be a hierarchy of responsibilities within that general supervisory category, and all supervisory tasks may not be rewarded equally. That is where the

---

[3] Hill (1980) finds this also—46% of the men and 27.3% of the women in her 1976 PSID sample consider themselves to be supervisors.

NLSY79 1996 data are very informative. They allow one to look beyond the supervisory "title" to examine types and levels of responsibilities associated with being in a supervisory role and their associated wage effects.

Why might wages vary with levels of supervisory responsibilities? In their textbook on compensation, Milkovich and Newman (1999) posit that establishment pay structures are usually defined by job levels, pay differentials between the levels, and criteria for determining the levels and pay differentials. Pay structures are thus hierarchical, with higher job levels associated with higher pay. The criteria for determining the job levels and pay differentials between levels may be job-based (based on job tasks, responsibilities, and expected behaviors and results) or person-based (based on skills (human capital), knowledge, and competencies). Both suggest that higher wages may be associated with jobs with higher-level supervisory responsibilities. In the first case, this can be due to the job content involving relatively higher authority and responsibility.[4] In the second case, this can be caused by more skilled/higher ability individuals filling jobs that include increased responsibilities.

The theoretical economics literature also provides some insights into why we could expect individuals with jobs with higher supervisory authority to earn higher wages. For example, Calvo and Wellisz (1979) and Rosen (1982) show a potential trickle down effect of supervisory decision-making. As individuals move up the establishment's hierarchy, they can have a direct or indirect influence on the productivity of the workers below them. Establishments will thus assign more talented and productive individuals to higher-level positions with greater responsibility and compensate them with higher wages.

---

[4] See Harvey (1990) for a description of job analysis, particularly his discussion of the measurement of dimensions of managerial jobs.

Establishments may use promotions into jobs with higher-level responsibilities and higher pay to reward workers for specific human capital accumulation (Carmichael, 1984). Tournament theory suggests that promotion into jobs with higher pay, prestige, and responsibility can be a mechanism to induce employee effort (Lazear and Rosen, 1981, and Rosen, 1986). At each level, employees 'compete' for a prize (higher position and pay). The more productive employee is then promoted to the next level, where he or she then competes for the next higher position, and so on.

The above scenarios predict rewards and responsibilities will rise with job level. This paper focuses on two different types of supervisory responsibilities: responsibility over subordinates' pay or promotions and responsibility over setting subordinates' job tasks. Could these two aspects of supervisory responsibility have wage implications beyond the effect of supervisory status? The above literature suggests it may. Whether due to job content, the ability and productivity of the job holder, or both, we would expect to see higher wage returns associated with higher levels of supervisory responsibility.

The goal of this paper is to examine empirically the nature and consequences of supervisory responsibility. There is a small empirical literature on supervisory authority and the wage returns to having this authority. Mostly from the sociology and industrial relations literature, and based on data from the 1970s or early 1980s, this literature shows a gender gap in supervisory status as seen with the GSS data, particularly with respect to higher levels of authority (Wolf and Fligstein (1979), Hill (1980), Reskin and Roos (1992)). The literature also (mostly) suggests a significant, positive wage effect associated with supervisory responsibility that is not statistically different for men and women (Ferber and Green (1991), Cannings (1988), Jacobs (1992)).

This paper adds to the existing literature in a number of ways. First, it uses recent data for a nationally representative sample of men and women. The NLSY79 data set also contains more extensive labor market information than most of the other data sets. This allows the construction of much more detailed measures that may be important predictors of supervisory responsibility (such as tenure, training, and an aptitude measure). Second, it focuses on and more fully explores the issue of what it means to be a supervisor, and what aspects of supervisory status have earnings implications. Third, it investigates the effects of supervisory status and upper-level supervisory responsibilities on individuals' advancement potential with their employers.

II. What Do Supervisors Do? Evidence from the NLSY79

The National Longitudinal Survey of Youth 1979 (NLSY79) is a sample of over 10,000 young men and women[5] who were initially interviewed in 1979, and who had been interviewed through 1996 at the time I began my analysis. A new series of questions on various aspects of supervision was added in 1996. A question that asks respondents whether they "supervise the work of other employees" is used to determine supervisory status. Respondents who are supervisors are then asked whether they have full, some, or no responsibility for deciding the pay or promotions of the people they supervise. Similarly, they are asked how much responsibility they have for deciding the specific tasks or jobs to be done by their subordinates. The respondents are also asked the number and gender of their subordinates. In 1996, respondents' ages ranged from 31 to 39. As mentioned above, the thirties are an interesting age range to examine with respect to supervisory responsibilities. At this age, many individuals are past the job shopping stage that tends to occur in the early to mid-twenties and on a more defined career path.

Table 2 shows the percentage of workers who supervise employees and measures of supervisors' authority. The subsample shown, which is that used for the analyses that follow, consists of 2,569 men and 2,057 women who were employed at least 30 hours per week, had hourly wages between $2 and $100, and were not self-employed or working without pay at their main job at the time of the 1996 interview. The hours restriction should eliminate some of the possible supervisory differential that could be due to a lesser attachment to the labor market. The remaining male and female employees may be more homogenous with respect to their labor market characteristics than has been seen in some of the previous investigations, which did not impose such restrictions.

Table 2 indicates, not surprisingly given what was found in the GSS data, that a large percentage of men and women report that they supervise the work of other employees (41.5% of men and 35.1% of women). Thus there is a 6.4 percentage point gender gap in supervision. The table shows differences in the extent of responsibility supervisors have over subordinates' pay or promotions and job tasks.[6] Only 20.8% of male supervisors and 13.4% of female supervisors report that they have full responsibility for deciding their subordinates' pay or promotions, while 38.7% of male supervisors and 43.1% of female supervisors report having no authority in this area of responsibility. On the other hand, most supervisors have at least some responsibility for setting their subordinates' job tasks; only about 6% of male and female supervisors report having no responsibility in that area. Control over subordinates' pay or promotions is probably a

---

[5] The NLSY79 includes oversamples of black and Hispanic individuals.
[6] Two separate questions asked about responsibility over subordinates' pay and promotions. Because the responses are so highly correlated (correlation coefficient of about .7) the two questions have been combined to form one variable.

higher grade of responsibility than that of setting employees' job tasks, and may be associated with a higher rung of the job ladder. The data also show that, on average, 23% of the employees supervised by men are female, while 73% of the employees supervised by women are female. This indicates significant gender segregation along supervisory lines.[7]

III. Variables

This paper seeks to address three main questions. The first is whether there are wage consequences associated with having different levels and types of supervisory authority. The second concerns factors affecting the likelihood of having supervisory status and higher-level supervisory responsibilities. The third asks whether having supervisory status or higher-level supervisory responsibilities affects the ability to advance with the current employer.

To examine the first question, log of hourly wage equations are estimated that include supervisory characteristics as regressors. One could make an endogeneity argument that certain types of individuals (higher ability, for example, as discussed in the literature review in section I.) are more likely to become supervisors. At the same time, it is very difficult to think of an instrument that affects the probability of becoming a supervisor (or having higher-level supervisory responsibilities) that is not correlated with the disturbance term in the wage equation. The very detailed nature of the NLSY79 data, however, allows for extensive controls (including an aptitude measure) that may help to mitigate this potential problem.

Probits of the probability of having supervisory authority, and conditioning on having supervisory authority, ordered probits of the probability of having higher levels of supervisory

---

[7] Reskin and Roos (1992), in their 1982 sample of managers in Illinois, found that 77% of female managers' highest ranking subordinates are women, and 24% of male managers' highest ranking subordinates are women.

7

authority (over employees' pay or promotions) are estimated to address the second question. Probit estimates of the probability that a future promotion is possible with the present employer (where supervisory characteristics are also included as regressors) are used to investigate the third question.

General background characteristics such as gender, race, ethnicity, years of education, and years of work experience all may influence the likelihood of becoming a supervisor. Based on previous research concerning supervision, we expect the variable female to have a negative impact. The same direction is predicted for the variables black and Hispanic. Years of education and years of experience and tenure are most likely positive predictors of supervisory status and higher-level supervisory responsibilities.[8] In addition, job and establishment-specific characteristics such as union status, establishment size, and job sector (public, private, or non-profit) may also have an impact. The structure of supervision may differ across industries and thus ten industry dummy variables are included in some specifications.[9] Having been recently promoted or having recently received training can increase the likelihood of becoming a supervisor and of having higher-level supervisory responsibilities.[10] Because people with higher aptitude may be more likely to have supervisory status, individuals' scores from the Armed Forces Qualifying Test (AFQT) are included in the analyses. The AFQT is a measure of math and verbal aptitude. Home responsibilities may influence the likelihood of having (and perhaps

---

[8] Experience equals the number of weeks worked (divided by 52) since the individual first left school for a period of 12 months or more. For individuals who left school prior to January 1, 1978—the first date for which employment data are available for many respondents—experience equals the number of weeks worked (divided by 52) since January 1, 1978. The results remain very similar when a dummy variable is included for this truncation, and thus the dummy variable is not included in the specifications shown in this paper. The majority (over 80%) of affected respondents are from the earliest birth years of the NLSY79, 1957-59, and are ages 18-20 as of January 1, 1978. Tenure equals the portion of experience that occurred with the current employer.

[9] Occupation controls are not included, as many occupations reflect supervisory status. For example, almost 1/3 of supervisors in this sample are managers and administrators, as compared to less than 1/20 of non-supervisors. However, for comparison purposes, notes throughout the empirical results sections state whether results changed with the addition of occupation dummy variables.

wanting to have) supervisory status. Thus variables indicating marital status, number of children, and presence of a child aged 6 or less are included. Indicators for urban location and for living in the South region are included. All of these variables are also in the promotion potential probits, and (excluding the indicators of home responsibilities) are also regressors in the wage equations.

Descriptive statistics are shown in Table 3. On average, men earn $15.00/hour while women earn $12.33/hour, a differential of about 18%. More men than women believe that they could receive a promotion by their present employer during the next two years. Men and women appear alike on a number of key background characteristics, including tenure and recent receipt of a promotion. However, women are much more likely to work in the non-profit sector, while men are more likely to work in the private sector. AFQT scores for men and women appear fairly similar. The test was administered to NLSY79 respondents in 1980 and because respondents were different ages when they took the test, the scores have been standardized by birth year to have a mean of zero and a standard deviation of one (following Neal and Johnson, 1996).[11]

IV. Wage Returns to Aspects of Supervision

The wage consequences of having supervisory status, and of having different levels of supervisory responsibilities are first examined. The findings will indicate whether supervisory responsibilities are associated with higher wages. The findings will also be used to test whether

---

[10] See Pergamit and Veum (1999).

[11] This standardization was done for the entire, weighted NLSY79 sample. Thus, the mean (standard deviation) here is not exactly zero (one), given that the data are unweighted and include oversamples of black and Hispanic individuals.

the returns to supervision vary by gender. If the meaning of supervisory status or upper-level supervisory responsibilities differs systematically for men and women, we would expect the wage returns to differ by gender.[12] However, as noted in the previous section, supervisory wage effects should be interpreted with some caution due to the potential endogeneity of the supervisor variables. In particular, if more talented/productive individuals are more likely to have supervisory responsibilities and if these attributes are not fully captured by the explanatory variables in the wage equations, then the supervisory wage effects could be overstated.

Tables 4 and 5 depict estimates from the hourly wage equations. Equations are first pooled for men and women (estimates shown in the first two columns of each table) and then estimated separately. The specifications in Table 4 include a measure of supervisory status, but no measures of particular supervisory responsibilities, while the specifications in Table 5 also control for supervisory responsibilities over subordinates' pay or promotions, and job tasks, the number of subordinates, and the gender composition of the group of subordinates. Specifications in even-numbered columns of both tables include a set of industry dummy variables.

The pooled equations in Tables 4 and 5 indicate that, even with extensive controls for human capital characteristics, being female is associated with about a -14 to -16% impact on wages [e.g., $(\exp(-.178) - 1)*100$].[13] Being black is associated with a significant and negative effect for men, but not for women. Higher levels of education, experience, tenure, and AFQT scores have the expected positive impact on wages, as does off-site training. Working in the

---

[12] Jacobs (1992) tests a similar hypothesis; he asks whether the rising number of women identified as managers in Census data is "real" or rather due to women being given the title of manager without increased wages and authority.

[13] The null hypothesis that the slope coefficients are the same for men and women is rejected for all specifications.

private sector has a positive impact on wages for men and women, while working in the non-profit sector has a negative effect for men only.[14]

Turning to the effects of supervisory status and responsibilities on wages, Table 4 shows that supervisory status has a significant, positive effect on wages of about 10 to 11% for men and about 6 to 9% for women; these effects are not statistically different for men and women. Table 5 shows that responsibility over pay or promotions is the aspect of supervision measured here that has very significant wage returns. Having full responsibility over subordinates' pay or promotions has about a 17 to 18% impact on wages for men and about 13 to 14% for women, depending on the specification. The wage return for having some responsibility over pay or promotions is also significant and positive.[15]

Levels of responsibility for setting job tasks, which is a duty most supervisors report having at least to some extent, have no effect on wages. The log of number of subordinates impacts wages for men, but only when industry controls are included (specifications in even-numbered columns).[16] However, when the variable was interacted with industry dummy variables neither the interactions nor the variable itself were statistically significant. This finding is not too surprising. On the one hand, all else equal, supervisors might be expected to be compensated more as they supervise more employees, because they may have a larger impact on the employer's profitability. However, the number of subordinates might also be related to hierarchical position. Supervisors lower down and higher up in the job hierarchy both may directly supervise the work of fewer employees, thus confounding a potential wage effect. The

---

[14] The omitted category is the public sector.
[15] The coefficients for full (some) responsibility over pay or promotions are not statistically different for men and women.
The wage impacts of levels of responsibility over subordinates' pay or promotions remain very similar when industry is disaggregated into 43 dummy variables.

results in Table 5 also indicate that there is no wage differential associated with the gender composition of the group of subordinates.[17]

To obtain a somewhat different perspective on the wage returns to being a supervisor, a look at the combined effects of supervisory variables is useful. Three cases are examined: (1) being a supervisor with full responsibility over subordinates' pay or promotions, and job tasks; (2) being a supervisor with some responsibility over subordinates' pay or promotions, and job tasks; (3) being a supervisor with no responsibility over subordinates' pay or promotions, and job tasks. Coefficients and standard errors for the three cases are shown below.[18]

	Males	Males	Females	Females
Case (1)	.204 (.030)	.209 (.029)	.149 (.039)	.166 (.039)
Case (2)	.113 (.028)	.130 (.027)	.083 (.030)	.112 (.029)
Case (3)	-.010 (.050)	.009 (.049)	-.045 (.058)	-.008 (.056)
Industry dummy vars.?	No	Yes	No	Yes

Note: Standard errors in ()s. Estimates computed from specifications shown in columns (3) through (6) of Table 5.

The results indicate that the payoff for being a supervisor lies in the types and levels of responsibilities, rather than in simply having supervisory 'status.' In addition, we cannot reject the hypothesis that men and women receive equal wage returns for these higher authority levels.

---

[16] The addition of 8 occupation dummy variables does not change this result, nor does the disaggregation of industry into 43 dummy variables. Also, when occupation dummy variables are included without industry dummy variables, the variable is not significant.

[17] Arrow (1985) suggests that if supervisors dislike supervising a certain type of employee (say female), a wage differential based on the proportion of female subordinates could arise. If the variable is associated with the nature of the occupation a wage effect might be expected to occur as well. No effect is found, however.

[18] The variables log of number of subordinates and proportion of subordinates who are female are evaluated at their mean (by gender) in all three cases. The delta-method was used to compute the standard errors.

V. The Likelihood of Being a Supervisor, and of Having Responsibility Over Subordinates' Pay

or Promotions

The previous section shows that supervisory responsibility over subordinates' pay or promotions is associated with high wage returns. To attain this high level of supervisory responsibility, it is necessary to attain general supervisory status. The next set of estimates is used to investigate who is more likely to attain supervisory status. It is followed by an examination of factors that affect the likelihood of having responsibility over subordinates' pay or promotions, conditional on supervising the work of others.

Table 6 shows probit estimates of the probability of supervising the work of others; marginal effects are in brackets.[19] Columns (1) and (2) show that being female has a negative and significant impact on the likelihood of being a supervisor of about -7 to -7.5%.[20] This suggests that women are less likely to attain this initial 'rung' of the supervisory job ladder. Being black also is associated with a negative impact for men and women, while being Hispanic is not associated with a significant effect. Years of education, tenure, and having been recently promoted have the expected positive impact on the likelihood of being a supervisor. Off-site training has a positive and significant effect for men only. Working in the non-profit sector has a strong positive impact for women only, of about 12%. Of the variables that relate to home responsibilities—married, number of children, and child aged 6 or less—none are significant for women, and the number of children is significant and positive for men.

---

[19] Marginal effects for dichotomous variables were calculated by taking the difference in the probability that the individual is a supervisor defined when the dichotomous variable equals 1 and equals 0 for each individual, and then averaging over the sample. Marginal effects for continuous variables were calculated by taking the derivative of the probability the individual is a supervisor with respect to the particular continuous variable, and then averaging over the sample (see Greene (1997)).

[20] The null hypothesis that the slope coefficients are the same for men and women is rejected for both specifications.

Table 7 displays ordered probit estimates of the probability of having responsibility over employees' pay or promotions (conditional on supervising the work of others).[21] Being female is associated with a small negative effect (under 3%) on the probability of having the highest level of responsibility over employees' pay or promotions, and is only marginally significant in the specification that includes industry dummy variables.[22] This finding suggests that once women obtain supervisory status, they do not appear to lag very much behind in attaining this higher 'rung' of the supervisory ladder. Being black is found not to be statistically significant, and being Hispanic is associated with a positive effect for women. A recent promotion is a positive predictor of the likelihood of having the highest level of responsibility over subordinates' pay or promotions, but recent training does not appear to be significant. In addition, indicators for home responsibilities are not statistically significant for men or women.[23]

VI. Promotion Potential

Once supervisory status and higher-level supervisory responsibilities are obtained, is it more difficult in general to advance further with the current employer? Are these upper-level

---

[21] Respondents can report having full, some, or no responsibility for deciding the pay or promotions of the people they supervise. The sign of the coefficient indicates the impact of that variable on the probability of having the highest level (full) of responsibility over employees' pay or promotions. −1 multiplied by the sign on the coefficient is the direction of impact of that variable on the probability of having no responsibility over subordinates' pay or promotions.
Marginal effects are for the probability that the individual has the highest level of responsibility over subordinates' pay or promotions, and are calculated in a similar manner (for continuous and dichotomous) as was described for the probability of being a supervisor.
[22] The null hypothesis that the slope coefficients are the same for men and women is not rejected for either specification.
When occupation controls are added, the coefficient on female is statistically significant (the marginal effect is -4.3% for the specification that excludes industry dummy variables and -3.5% for the specification that includes industry dummy variables).
[23] Results with respect to determinants of other supervisory outcomes (log of number of subordinates, proportion of subordinates who are female, responsibility for setting subordinates' job tasks) are available from the author upon request.

supervisory responsibilities an indicator that people are reaching the top of their job hierarchy? The variable used to address these queries is the response to a question that asks individuals whether a promotion is possible with their current employer within the next two years. Thus whether individuals believe that they are "stuck" at various levels in the supervisory hierarchy can be examined. Table 3 shows that 61.5% of men and 55.2% of women believe a promotion is possible with their present employer within the next two years. Of the individuals who believe no further promotion is possible, about 70% of men and 64% of women choose "no further promotion potential" as the reason, which suggests that they believe they have gone as far as they can with their present employer.[24]

Tables 8 and 9 display probit estimates of the probability of responding that a promotion is possible within the next two years. The specifications in Table 8 include a measure of supervisory status, but no additional measures of supervisory responsibilities, while the specifications in Table 9 include measures of supervisory responsibilities as well. The results in both tables indicate that women are about 6% less likely to respond that a promotion is possible.[25] Table 8 shows that supervisory status is positively related to the probability a promotion is possible within the next two years for both women and men. This positive relationship suggests that it is not more difficult to be promoted once general supervisory status is obtained. When levels of supervisory responsibility are included in the specifications (Table 9), it does not appear that promotion potential decreases for either women or men as they move up the supervisory hierarchy.

---

[24] Other responses for lack of promotion potential include: someone from above must leave (the next most common response), additional education/training is needed, company reorganization, and change in company ownership.
[25] The null hypothesis that the slope coefficients are the same for men and women is rejected for all specifications in Tables 8 and 9.

The impact of race is also interesting: black individuals are significantly more likely to respond that a promotion is possible with their present employer. Recent promotion also has a significant positive impact on the probability of stating a future promotion is possible with the current employer for both men and women. Pergamit and Veum (1999) find that a recent promotion is a strong (positive) predictor of a current promotion. They suggest that this may occur because certain jobs or employers tend to have more of a hierarchical structure than others, which would generate this effect.[26] This is also a possible explanation for the positive impact of supervisory status on promotion potential. Perhaps workers employed in organizations that are more hierarchically structured are more likely to have supervisory responsibility, and also have more potential for advancement with their employer.

VII. Conclusion

There is little empirical literature about supervisors—who they are, what they do, and whether there are economic rewards to having this authority. Yet supervisory status and upper-level supervisory responsibilities are an important part of individuals' jobs, and the attainment of this authority can mark advancements along a career path. This paper examines what it means to be a supervisor, in terms of what types of responsibilities are associated with supervisory status of men and women, who is more likely to have this authority, and what are the wage and advancement consequences from having these levels of responsibilities. A new series of questions on aspects of supervision added to the 1996 interview of the National Longitudinal Survey of Youth 1979 (NLSY79) makes possible the empirical investigation of these issues.

---

[26] They also point out that past promotion may be an indicator for worker motivation, which would also predict this effect.

16

The NLSY79 data show that about 42% of male and 35% of female full-time workers consider themselves to be supervisors. This fairly high incidence of supervisory authority is also found in other data sets, such as the General Social Surveys (GSS) (See Table 1). About 21% of male supervisors and 13% of female supervisors report full responsibility for deciding subordinates' pay or promotions. While a large percentage, about 39% of male supervisors and 43% of female supervisors, report having no responsibility in this area, most supervisors have at least some responsibility over setting subordinates' job tasks.

Supervisory status does have a sizable wage return for both men and women, of about 9-10%. However, the addition of supervisory responsibilities and the number and gender of subordinates to specifications shows that responsibility over subordinates' pay or promotions is the aspect of supervision that has large, significant wage returns. Having supervisory status without upper-level supervisory responsibilities is found to have no wage returns. Thus it appears that the monetary rewards to supervision are not associated with simply having supervisory "status" or a supervisory title, per se, but rather from having associated upper-level supervisory responsibilities.

The empirical analyses show some interesting results with respect to gender. Men and women are not compensated significantly differently for having supervisory status or upper-level supervisory responsibilities. Women are, however, about 7% less likely to have supervisory status, and, conditional on having supervisory status, marginally less likely to have upper-level responsibility over subordinates' pay or promotions. It appears that once women attain supervisory status, there is a small associated responsibility differential for these mid-career supervisors.

References

Arrow, Kenneth J. 1985. "Some Mathematical Models of Race Discrimination in the Labor Market." In <u>Collected Papers of Kenneth J. Arrow, Vol. 6</u>. Cambridge, MA: Belknap Press., pp. 112-29.

Athey, Susan, Christopher Avery, and Peter Zemsky. forthcoming. "Mentoring and Diversity." <u>American Economic Review</u>.

Calvo, Guillermo A., and Stanislaw Wellisz. 1979. "Hierarchy, Ability, and Income Distribution." <u>Journal of Political Economy</u>, Vol. 87, No. 5, pp. 991-1010.

Cannings, Kathy. 1988. "The Earnings of Female and Male Middle Managers: A Canadian Case Study." <u>Journal of Human Resources</u>, Vol. 23, No. 1, pp. 34-56.

Carmichael, Lorne. 1983. "Firm-Specific Human Capital and Promotion Ladders." <u>Bell Journal of Economics</u>, Vol. 14, No. 1, pp. 251-58.

Ferber, Marianne A., and Carol A. Green. 1991. "Occupational Segregation and the Earnings Gap: Further Evidence." In Emily P. Hoffman, ed., <u>Essays on the Economics of Discrimination</u>. Kalamazoo: W.E. Upjohn Institute for Employment Research, pp. 145-65.

Gardecki, Rosella, and David Neumark. 1998. "Order from Chaos? The Effects of Early Labor Market Experiences on Adult Labor Market Outcomes." <u>Industrial and Labor Relations Review</u>, Vol. 51, No. 2, pp. 299-322.

Greene, William H. 1997. <u>Econometric Analysis</u>. 3rd edition. New Jersey: Prentice Hall.

Harvey, Robert J. 1991. "Job Analysis." In Marvin D. Dunnette and Leaetta M. Hough, eds., Handbook of Industrial and Organizational Psychology. 2nd edition. Palo Alto: Consulting Psychologists Press, Inc., pp. 71-163.

Hill, Martha S. 1980. "Authority at Work: How Men and Women Differ." In G. Duncan and J. Morgan, eds., Five Thousand American Families, Vol. 8. Ann Arbor: University of Michigan Press, pp. 107-46.

Jacobs, Jerry A. 1992. "Women's Entry into Management: Trends in Earnings, Authority, and Values among Salaried Managers." Administrative Science Quarterly, Vol. 37, pp. 282-301.

Lazear, Edward P., and Sherwin Rosen. 1981. "Rank-Order Tournaments as Optimum Labor Contracts." Journal of Political Economy, Vol. 89, No. 5, pp. 841-64.

Leonard, Jonathan S. 1987. "Carrots and Sticks: Pay, Supervision, and Turnover." Journal of Labor Economics, Vol. 5, No. 4, part 2, pp. S136-52.

Milkovich, George T., and Jerry M. Newman. 1999. Compensation. NY: The McGraw-Hill Companies, Inc.

Neal, Derek A., and William R. Johnson. 1996. "The Role of Premarket Factors in Black-White Wage Differences." Journal of Political Economy, Vol. 104, No. 5, pp. 869-95.

Pergamit, Michael R., and Jonathan R. Veum. 1999. "What Is a Promotion?" Industrial and Labor Relations Review, Vol. 52, No. 4, pp. 581-601.

Prendergast, Canice J. 1995. "A Theory of Responsibility in Organizations." Journal of Labor Economics, Vol. 13, No. 3, pp. 387-400.

Reskin, Barbara F., and Catherine E. Roos. 1992. "Jobs, Authority, and Earnings among Managers." Work and Occupations, Vol. 19, No. 4, pp. 342-65.

Rosen, Sherwin. 1982. "Authority, Control, and the Distribution of Earnings." <u>Bell Journal of</u>

    <u>Economics</u>, Vol. 13, No. 2, pp. 311-23.

Rosen, Sherwin. 1986. "Prizes and Incentives in Elimination Tournaments." <u>American</u>

    <u>Economic Review</u>, Vol. 76, No. 4, pp. 701-15.

Wolf, Wendy C., and Neil D. Fligstein. 1979. "Sex and Authority in the Workplace: The

    Causes of Sexual Inequality." <u>American Sociological Review</u>, Vol. 44, pp. 235-52.

Table 1. Percentage of Full-Time, Non Self-Employed Workers Who Directly Supervise Employees

	Workers Ages 18-65 Years		
	1970s	1980s	1990s
All	39.0	43.5	41.3
N	2,722	3,596	2,916
Males	41.8	46.3	44.2
N	1,762	1,987	1,546
Females	33.9	40.0	38.0
N	960	1,609	1,370
	Workers Ages 31-39 Years		
	1970s	1980s	1990s
All	43.6	48.7	44.3
N	557	1,021	849
Males	47.0	52.9	48.1
N	362	586	466
Females	37.4	43.0	39.7
N	195	435	383

Note: The years of data included above are: 1972-74, 1976-77, 1980, 1982, 1984-85, 1987-89, 1990-91, 1993-94, and 1996.
Source: General Social Surveys (GSS) Data, 1972-1996

Table 2. Percentage of Workers Who Are Supervisors and Descriptive Statistics of Supervisory Characteristics

	All	Males	Females
Percentage with supervisory status	38.7	41.5	35.1
N full sample	4,626	2,569	2,057
Among supervisors, percentage with:			
Full responsibility for subordinates' pay or promotions	17.8	20.8	13.4
Some responsibility for subordinates' pay or promotions	41.7	40.5	43.5
No responsibility for subordinates' pay or promotions	40.5	38.7	43.1
Full responsibility for setting subordinates' job tasks	54.4	57.4	50.0
Some responsibility for setting subordinates' job tasks	39.7	36.6	44.3
No responsibility for setting subordinates' job tasks	5.9	6.0	5.7
Additional supervisory characteristics:			
Log of number of subordinates	1.654 (1.129)	1.739 (1.130)	1.528 (1.116)
Proportion of subordinates who are female	.434 (.402)	.233 (.314)	.733 (.325)
N supervisors	1,789	1,067	722

Note: Means, standard deviations in ( )s. Data are restricted to those who are not self-employed or working without pay, and who work at least 30 hours per week. Respondents are ages 31-39 in 1996.
Source: National Longitudinal Survey of Youth 1979 (NLSY79) Data, 1996

Table 3. Descriptive Statistics

	All	Males	Females
Hourly wage	13.812 (7.787)	15.000 (8.496)	12.327 (6.501)
Log of hourly wage	2.498 (.496)	2.580 (.499)	2.396 (.474)
Believe a promotion is possible in next two years	.587	.615	.552
Female	.445	.000	1.000
Black	.299	.286	.316
Hispanic	.182	.180	.185
Years of education	13.299 (2.360)	13.123 (2.423)	13.520 (2.259)
AFQT score	-.212 (1.016)	-.199 (1.074)	-.229 (.939)
Experience (years)	12.473 (3.572)	12.843 (3.412)	12.011 (3.712)
Experience squared/10	16.833 (8.344)	17.657 (8.207)	15.803 (8.401)
Tenure (years)	5.355 (4.715)	5.320 (4.754)	5.398 (4.666)
Tenure squared/10	5.090 (7.285)	5.090 (7.370)	5.090 (7.180)
Promotion in last two years	.220	.219	.222
On-site seminar or training program in last two years	.182	.169	.198
Off-site seminar or training program in last two years	.068	.056	.083
Private sector	.766	.823	.695
Non-profit sector	.067	.045	.094
Union status	.214	.224	.201
Log of establishment size	4.151 (2.026)	4.004 (2.052)	4.335 (1.979)

Table 3 continued

Marital status	.571	.598	.539
Number of children	1.310 (1.231)	1.211 (1.271)	1.435 (1.168)
Child aged 6 or less	.350	.376	.317
N	4,626	2,569	2,057

Note: Means, standard deviations in ( )s.

Table 4. OLS Log of Hourly Wage Equation Estimates

	All (1)	All (2)	Males (3)	Males (4)	Females (5)	Females (6)
Supervisory Status	**.076** **(.012)**	**.098** **(.012)**	**.093** **(.017)**	**.106** **(.016)**	**.057** **(.017)**	**.085** **(.017)**
Female	-.178 (.012)	-.154 (.012)	----	----	----	----
Black	-.050 (.016)	-.046 (.015)	-.107 (.022)	-.098 (.021)	.017 (.022)	.017 (.022)
Hispanic	.012 (.016)	.007 (.016)	-.028 (.022)	-.028 (.022)	.063 (.023)	.054 (.023)
Years of education	.061 (.003)	.059 (.003)	.057 (.004)	.057 (.004)	.064 (.005)	.061 (.005)
AFQT score	.097 (.008)	.095 (.008)	.088 (.011)	.086 (.010)	.111 (.012)	.108 (.012)
Experience (years)	.028 (.008)	.023 (.008)	.024 (.012)	.020 (.012)	.031 (.011)	.029 (.011)
Experience squared/10	-.002 (.004)	-.001 (.003)	-.001 (.005)	.001 (.005)	-.004 (.005)	-.004 (.005)
Tenure (years)	.031 (.004)	.031 (.004)	.031 (.006)	.033 (.005)	.029 (.006)	.028 (.006)
Tenure squared/10	-.013 (.003)	-.013 (.003)	-.014 (.004)	-.014 (.003)	-.011 (.004)	-.010 (.004)
Promotion in last two years	.026 (.014)	.027 (.014)	.042 (.019)	.041 (.019)	.007 (.020)	.010 (.019)
On-site seminar or training program in last two years	.041 (.015)	.034 (.015)	.048 (.022)	.042 (.021)	.032 (.021)	.024 (.020)
Off-site seminar or training program in last two years	.087 (.023)	.080 (.022)	.088 (.035)	.084 (.034)	.099 (.029)	.086 (.029)
Private sector	.077 (.017)	.086 (.020)	.094 (.025)	.116 (.032)	.060 (.023)	.059 (.026)
Non-profit sector	-.051 (.026)	-.057 (.025)	-.130 (.043)	-.127 (.042)	-.010 (.032)	-.017 (.032)
Union status	.150 (.015)	.137 (.015)	.180 (.021)	.160 (.020)	.109 (.023)	.106 (.023)

Table 4 continued

Log of establishment size	.035 (.003)	.033 (.003)	.035 (.004)	.036 (.004)	.035 (.004)	.030 (.004)
Intercept	1.056 (.066)	1.117 (.072)	1.145 (.098)	1.155 (.103)	.804 (.090)	.912 (.105)
Industry dummy vars.?	No	Yes	No	Yes	No	Yes
N	4,626	4,626	2,569	2,569	2,057	2,057
Adjusted R-Squared	.418	.453	.389	.427	.424	.453

Note: Standard errors in ( )s. Also included in equations are indicators for urban location and South region.

Table 5. OLS Log of Hourly Wage Equation Estimates (Includes Supervisory Responsibility Variables)

	All (1)	All (2)	Males (3)	Males (4)	Females (5)	Females (6)
Supervisory Status	**-.008 (.041)**	**-.021 (.039)**	**-.013 (.052)**	**-.033 (.051)**	**-.017 (.068)**	**.003 (.066)**
Full responsibility for subordinates' pay or promotions	**.157 (.029)**	**.148 (.028)**	**.169 (.038)**	**.157 (.037)**	**.132 (.047)**	**.118 (.046)**
Some responsibility for subordinates' pay or promotions	**.088 (.021)**	**.088 (.021)**	**.100 (.029)**	**.100 (.028)**	**.072 (.031)**	**.073 (.031)**
Full responsibility for setting subordinates' job tasks	**.054 (.041)**	**.052 (.039)**	**.046 (.054)**	**.044 (.052)**	**.062 (.062)**	**.056 (.061)**
Some responsibility for setting subordinates' job tasks	**.038 (.040)**	**.035 (.039)**	**.023 (.053)**	**.021 (.051)**	**.056 (.060)**	**.047 (.059)**
Log of number of subordinates	**-.004 [a] (.084)**	**.015 (.008)**	**.006 (.011)**	**.021 (.011)**	**-.006 (.013)**	**.004 (.012)**
Proportion of subordinates who are female	**-.043 (.024)**	**-.011 (.024)**	**-.034 (.040)**	**.019 (.039)**	**-.025 (.042)**	**-.024 (.041)**
Female	-.167 (.012)	-.148 (.012)	----	----	----	----
Black	-.049 (.015)	-.045 (.015)	-.105 (.022)	-.096 (.021)	.016 (.022)	.016 (.022)
Hispanic	.011 (.016)	.005 (.016)	-.028 (.022)	-.027 (.022)	.060 (.023)	.050 (.023)
Years of education	.059 (.003)	.057 (.003)	.056 (.005)	.055 (.004)	.063 (.005)	.060 (.005)
AFQT score	.095 (.008)	.093 (.008)	.086 (.011)	.084 (.010)	.109 (.012)	.106 (.012)
Experience (years)	.028 (.008)	.024 (.008)	.024 (.012)	.021 (.012)	.030 (.011)	.028 (.011)
Experience squared/10	-.003 (.004)	-.002 (.003)	-.001 (.005)	-.001 [a] (.050)	-.004 (.005)	-.004 (.005)
Tenure (years)	.030 (.004)	.030 (.004)	.029 (.006)	.031 (.005)	.029 (.006)	.028 (.006)
Tenure squared/10	-.012 (.003)	-.012 (.003)	-.013 (.004)	-.014 (.003)	-.011 (.004)	-.010 (.004)

Table 5 continued

Promotion in last two years	.019 (.014)	.019 (.014)	.034 (.019)	.033 (.019)	.002 (.020)	.003 (.019)
On-site seminar or training program in last two years	.041 (.015)	.034 (.015)	.048 (.022)	.042 (.021)	.031 (.021)	.023 (.020)
Off-site seminar or training program in last two years	.083 (.023)	.074 (.022)	.082 (.034)	.076 (.033)	.095 (.029)	.083 (.029)
Private sector	.067 (.017)	.078 (.020)	.079 (.025)	.102 (.032)	.054 (.023)	.056 (.026)
Non-profit sector	-.053 (.026)	-.061 (.025)	-.136 (.043)	-.136 (.042)	-.014 (.032)	-.021 (.032)
Union status	.157 (.015)	.144 (.015)	.190 (.021)	.171 (.020)	.113 (.023)	.109 (.023)
Log of establishment size	.035 (.003)	.033 (.003)	.035 (.004)	.035 (.004)	.036 (.004)	.030 (.004)
Intercept	1.087 (.067)	1.157 (.072)	1.190 (.098)	1.207 (.103)	.832 (.090)	.948 (.106)
Industry dummy vars.?	No	Yes	No	Yes	No	Yes
N	4,626	4,626	2,569	2,569	2,057	2,057
Adjusted R-Squared	.424	.460	.396	.436	.426	.455

Note: Standard errors in ( )s. Also included in equations are indicators for urban location and South region.
[a] Coefficient and standard error have been multiplied by 10.

Table 6. Probit Estimates of the Probability of Supervising the Work of Others

	All (1)	All (2)	Males (3)	Males (4)	Females (5)	Females (6)
Female	-.205 (.041) [-.070]	-.224 (.044) [-.076]	----	----	----	----
Black	-.162 (.056) [-.055]	-.152 (.056) [-.051]	-.148 (.075) [-.051]	-.128 (.076) [-.043]	-.180 (.085) [-.060]	-.178 (.086) [-.059]
Hispanic	-.076 (.057) [-.026]	-.055 (.058) [-.018]	-.059 (.076) [-.020]	-.047 (.077) [-.016]	-.095 (.087) [-.032]	-.063 (.088) [-.021]
Years of education	.067 (.011) [.023]	.073 (.012) [.025]	.076 (.015) [.026]	.079 (.016) [.027]	.049 (.018) [.017]	.058 (.018) [.019]
AFQT score	.019 (.028) [.006]	.024 (.028) [.008]	.021 (.036) [.007]	.032 (.037) [.011]	.002 (.044) [-.001]	.007 (.045) [.002]
Experience (years)	.026 (.030) [.009]	.027 (.030) [.009]	.013[a] (.428) [.004]	-.004 (.043) [-.001]	.068 (.043) [.023]	.070 (.044) [.023]
Experience squared/10	-.006 (.013) [-.002]	-.006 (.013) [-.002]	.006 (.018) [.002]	.008 (.018) [.003]	-.026 (.019) [-.009]	-.024 (.019) [-.008]
Tenure (years)	.091 (.014) [.031]	.094 (.014) [.032]	.105 (.019) [.036]	.109 (.019) [.037]	.066 (.022) [.022]	.068 (.022) [.023]
Tenure squared/10	-.035 (.009) [-.012]	-.036 (.009) [-.012]	-.040 (.012) [-.014]	-.041 (.012) [-.001]	-.025 (.014) [-.008]	-.026 (.014) [-.009]
Promotion in last two years	.680 (.047) [.247]	.673 (.048) [.241]	.655 (.065) [.234]	.651 (.065) [.229]	.708 (.070) [.260]	.699 (.071) [.250]
On-site seminar or training program in last two years	.069 (.053) [.024]	.089 (.053) [.030]	.037 (.074) [.013]	.064 (.074) [.022]	.091 (.076) [.031]	.107 (.077) [.036]
Off-site seminar or training program in last two years	.235 (.078) [.083]	.245 (.079) [.085]	.373 (.118) [.131]	.373 (.118) [.129]	.154 (.106) [.054]	.189 (.107) [.064]

Table 6 continued

Private sector	.114	.125	.081	.146	.152	.146
	(.061)	(.074)	(.087)	(.114)	(.087)	(.101)
	[.039]	[.042]	[.028]	[.049]	[.051]	[.048]
Non-profit sector	.122	.132	-.170	-.164	.340	.350
	(.092)	(.092)	(.150)	(.150)	(.119)	(.119)
	[.043]	[.045]	[-.057]	[-.054]	[.120]	[.121]
Union status	-.457	-.447	-.610	-.607	-.239	-.222
	(.055)	(.056)	(.073)	(.074)	(.087)	(.089)
	[-.152]	[-.146]	[-.203]	[-.199]	[-.079]	[-.072]
Log of establishment size	-.066	-.049	-.057	-.039	-.077	-.059
	(.010)	(.011)	(.014)	(.015)	(.016)	(.016)
	[-.023]	[-.016]	[-.020]	[-.013]	[-.026]	[-.019]
Marital status	.026	.043	.046	.072	-.008 [a]	.005
	(.047)	(.047)	(.069)	(.069)	(.652)	(.066)
	[.009]	[.015]	[.016]	[.024]	[-.003]	[.002]
Number of children	.048	.043	.059	.058	.016	.007
	(.020)	(.020)	(.028)	(.028)	(.030)	(.031)
	[.017]	[.015]	[.020]	[.019]	[.005]	[.002]
Child aged 6 or less	-.078	-.071	-.089	-.094	-.066	-.046
	(.049)	(.049)	(.069)	(.070)	(.071)	(.072)
	[-.027]	[-.024]	[-.030]	[-.032]	[-.022]	[-.015]
Intercept	-1.473	-1.913	-1.518	-1.981	-1.536	-1.920
	(.243)	(.274)	(.341)	(.377)	(.361)	(.432)
Industry dummy vars.?	No	Yes	No	Yes	No	Yes
N	4,626	4,626	2,569	2,569	2,057	2,057
log likelihood	-2,793	-2,746	-1,549	1,524	-1,229	-1,200

Note: Standard errors in ( )s, marginal effects in [ ]s. Also included in equations are indicators for urban location and South region.

[a] Coefficient, standard error, and marginal effect have been multiplied by 10.

Table 7. Ordered Probit Estimates of the Probability of Having Responsibility over Subordinates' Pay or Promotions (Conditional on Supervising the Work of Others)

	All (1)	All (2)	Males (3)	Males (4)	Females (5)	Females (6)
Female	-.119 (.058) [-.029]	-.102 (.061) [-.024]	----	----	----	----
Black	-.046 (.080) [-.011]	-.059 (.081) [-.014]	-.055 (.104) [-.015]	-.073 (.105) [-.019]	-.036 (.128) [-.007]	-.046 (.129) [-.009]
Hispanic	.070 (.079) [.017]	.089 (.079) [.022]	-.005 (.103) [-.001]	-.005 (.103) [-.001]	.198 (.125) [.042]	.260 (.127) [.055]
Years of education	.088 (.016) [.021]	.096 (.016) [.023]	.084 (.020) [.022]	.093 (.021) [.024]	.091 (.026) [.018]	.103 (.026) [.020]
AFQT score	.058 (.040) [.014]	.058 (.040) [.014]	.050 (.051) [.013]	.039 (.052) [.010]	.065 (.064) [.013]	.073 (.065) [.014]
Experience (years)	.080 (.047) [.019]	.081 (.047) [.019]	.034 (.061) [.009]	.026 (.062) [.007]	.146 (.076) [.029]	.147 (.076) [.029]
Experience squared/10	-.012 (.020) [-.003]	-.013 (.020) [-.003]	.006 (.025) [.001]	.008 (.025) [.002]	-.039 (.032) [-.008]	-.040 (.033) [-.008]
Tenure (years)	.043 (.020) [.010]	.042 (.020) [.010]	.053 (.026) [.014]	.050 (.026) [.013]	.025 (.033) [.005]	.024 (.033) [.005]
Tenure squared/10	-.021 (.013) [-.005]	-.020 (.013) [-.005]	-.025 (.016) [-.007]	-.022 (.016) [-.006]	-.014 (.021) [-.003]	-.013 (.021) [-.002]
Promotion in last two years	.263 (.059) [.066]	.256 (.059) [.064]	.250 (.078) [.069]	.252 (.078) [.068]	.302 (.093) [.063]	.304 (.094) [.062]
On-site seminar or training program in last two years	.004[a] (.695) [.001]	.010[a] (.698) [.002]	-.011 (.092) [-.003]	-.017 (.093) [-.005]	.013 (.107) [.003]	.020 (.108) [.004]
Off-site seminar or training program in last two years	.147 (.096) [.037]	.167 (.097) [.042]	.143 (.131) [.040]	.124 (.132) [.034]	.170 (.142) [.037]	.218 (.145) [.046]

Table 7 continued

Private sector	.493	.310	.521	.389	.497	.268
	(.090)	(.106)	(.123)	(.152)	(.136)	(.154)
	[.104]	[.068]	[.119]	[.092]	[.089]	[.049]
Non-profit sector	.270	.263	.285	.251	.290	.290
	(.132)	(.132)	(.219)	(.220)	(.175)	(.175)
	[.071]	[.069]	[.083]	[.072]	[.065]	[.063]
Union status	-.445	-.439	-.533	-.534	-.304	-.290
	(.090)	(.091)	(.117)	(.118)	(.145)	(.146)
	[-.092]	[-.091]	[-.120]	[-.119]	[-.054]	[-.051]
Log of establishment size	-.036	-.029	-.041	-.038	-.028	-.011
	(.015)	(.015)	(.019)	(.020)	(.024)	(.025)
	[-.009]	[-.007]	[-.011]	[-.010]	[-.006]	[-.002]
Marital status	.066	.056	.054	.059	.083	.062
	(.066)	(.067)	(.094)	(.095)	(.097)	(.098)
	[.016]	[.013]	[.014]	[.015]	[.017]	[.012]
Number of children	-.006	.012[b]	-.021	-.013	.016	.029
	(.028)	(2.770)	(.037)	(.037)	(.044)	(.045)
	[-.001]	[.003]	[-.006]	[-.003]	[.003]	[.006]
Child aged 6 or less	-.045	-.032	-.015	-.012	-.060	-.025
	(.067)	(.067)	(.089)	(.089)	(.104)	(.106)
	[-.011]	[-.008]	[-.004]	[-.003]	[-.012]	[-.005]
Industry dummy vars.?	No	Yes	No	Yes	No	Yes
N	1,789	1,789	1,067	1,067	722	722
log likelihood	-1,741	-1,731	-1,062	-1,054	-672	-659

Note: Standard errors in ( )s, marginal effects for the probability of having the highest level of supervisory responsibility are in [ ]s. Also included in equations are indicators for urban location and South region.
[a] Coefficient, standard error, and marginal effect have been multiplied by 10.
[b] Coefficient, standard error, and marginal effect have been multiplied by 100.

Table 8. Probit Estimates of the Probability that a Promotion Is Possible in the Next Two Years

	All (1)	All (2)	Males (3)	Males (4)	Females (5)	Females (6)
Supervisory status	**.180**	**.173**	**.211**	**.214**	**.135**	**.117**
	(.042)	**(.043)**	**(.057)**	**(.058)**	**(.064)**	**(.065)**
	[.064]	**[.061]**	**[.074]**	**[.074]**	**[.048]**	**[.041]**
Female	-.179	-.184	----	----	----	----
	(.041)	(.043)				
	[-.064]	[-.065]				
Black	.316	.312	.278	.270	.362	.358
	(.055)	(.056)	(.075)	(.075)	(.084)	(.084)
	[.111]	[.109]	[.096]	[.092]	[.129]	[.126]
Hispanic	.117	.131	.102	.117	.136	.136
	(.056)	(.057)	(.076)	(.076)	(.085)	(.086)
	[.041]	[.046]	[.035]	[.040]	[.048]	[.048]
Years of education	.005	.007	.032	.031	-.027	-.023
	(.011)	(.012)	(.015)	(.016)	(.017)	(.018)
	[.002]	[.002]	[.011]	[.011]	[-.010]	[-.008]
AFQT score	-.017	-.023	-.064	-.072	.038	.031
	(.028)	(.028)	(.036)	(.036)	(.044)	(.044)
	[-.006]	[-.008]	[-.022]	[-.025]	[.013]	[.011]
Experience (years)	.030	.031	.020	.024	.050	.049
	(.029)	(.029)	(.042)	(.042)	(.040)	(.040)
	[.011]	[.011]	[.007]	[.008]	[.018]	[.017]
Experience squared/10	-.013	-.014	-.007	-.008	-.024	-.024
	(.012)	(.012)	(.018)	(.018)	(.018)	(.018)
	[-.005]	[-.005]	[-.002]	[-.003]	[-.008]	[-.009]
Tenure (years)	-.107	-.106	-.123	-.122	-.098	-.093
	(.014)	(.014)	(.019)	(.019)	(.022)	(.022)
	[-.038]	[-.037]	[-.043]	[-.042]	[-.035]	[-.033]
Tenure squared/10	.048	.047	.055	.054	.044	.041
	(.009)	(.009)	(.012)	(.012)	(.014)	(.014)
	[.017]	[.017]	[.019]	[.019]	[.016]	[.015]

Table 8 continued

Promotion in last two years	.452 (.050) [.157]	.439 (.051) [.152]	.364 (.069) [.125]	.358 (.069) [.122]	.546 (.075) [.192]	.532 (.075) [.186]
On-site seminar or training program in last two years	.313 (.054) [.109]	.311 (.054) [.108]	.440 (.078) [.148]	.450 (.078) [.150]	.175 (.076) [.062]	.164 (.076) [.058]
Off-site seminar or training program in last two years	-.022 (.078) [-.008]	.0124 [a] (.789) [.004]	-.015 (.118) [-.005]	-.020 (.119) [-.007]	-.019 (.106) [-.007]	.020 (.108) [.007]
Private sector	.087 (.059) [.031]	-.044 (.072) [-.015]	-.013 (.086) [-.004]	-.106 (.112) [-.036]	.155 (.084) [.056]	.005 (.098) [.002]
Non-profit sector	-.084 (.090) [-.030]	-.091 (.091) [-.032]	-.190 (.146) [-.068]	-.188 (.146) [-.066]	-.007 (.118) [-.002]	-.017 (.119) [-.006]
Union status	-.002 (.054) [-.001]	.019 (.054) [.007]	.029 (.071) [.010]	.048 (.072) [.016]	-.004 (.084) [-.001]	.011 (.085) [.004]
Log of establishment size	.117 (.010) [.041]	.119 (.011) [.042]	.105 (.014) [.037]	.100 (.015) [.035]	.128 (.016) [.046]	.139 (.017) [.049]
Marital status	.056 (.046) [.020]	.055 (.046) [.020]	.144 (.068) [.050]	.152 (.069) [.053]	-.036 (.064) [-.013]	-.043 (.064) [-.015]
Number of children	-.052 (.020) [-.019]	-.051 (.020) [-.018]	-.071 (.028) [-.025]	-.072 (.028) [-.025]	-.060 (.029) [-.022]	-.055 (.030) [-.019]
Child aged 6 or less	.150 (.048) [.053]	.151 (.048) [.053]	.202 (.069) [.070]	.197 (.069) [.068]	.088 (.069) [.031]	.097 (.070) [.034]
Intercept	-.657 (.235)	-.587 (.262)	-.805 (.336)	-.845 (.365)	-.615 (.344)	-.310 (.411)
Industry dummy vars.?	No	Yes	No	Yes	No	Yes
N	4,626	4,626	2,569	2,569	2,057	2,057
log likelihood	-2,877	-2,860	-1,571	-1,562	-1,286	-1,270

Note: Standard errors in ( )s, marginal effects in [ ]s. Also included in equations are indicators for urban location and South region.

[a] Coefficient, standard error, and marginal effect have been multiplied by 10.

Table 9. Probit Estimates of the Probability that a Promotion Is Possible in the Next Two Years (Includes Supervisory Responsibility Variables)

	All (1)	All (2)	Males (3)	Males (4)	Females (5)	Females (6)
Supervisory status	.178 (.143) [.063]	.188 (.144) [.066]	.373 (.189) [.128]	.394 (.191) [.134]	-.063 (.248) [-.023]	-.105 (.250) [-.037]
Full responsibility for subordinates' pay or promotions	.156 (.102) [.054]	.152 (.103) [.053]	.161 (.129) [.055]	.175 (.130) [.059]	.146 (.173) [.052]	.117 (.174) [.041]
Some responsibility for subordinates' pay or promotions	.178 (.075) [.062]	.181 (.075) [.063]	.155 (.099) [.053]	.171 (.100) [.058]	.200 (.115) [.071]	.167 (.116) [.058]
Full responsibility for setting subordinates' job tasks	-.153 (.144) [-.055]	-.147 (.144) [-.052]	-.442 (.195) [-.154]	-.444 (.196) [-.154]	.237 (.226) [.083]	.270 (.228) [.094]
Some responsibility for setting subordinates' job tasks	-.043 (.141) [-.015]	-.035 (.142) [-.012]	-.240 (.192) [-.084]	-.243 (.194) [-.085]	.229 (.220) [.080]	.258 (.221) [.089]
Log of number of subordinates	.025 (.030) [.009]	.013 (.030) [.005]	.060 (.040) [.021]	.050 (.041) [.017]	-.029 (.047) [-.010]	-.043 (.047) [-.015]
Proportion of subordinates who are female	-.074 (.085) [-.026]	-.089 (.086) [-.031]	-.043 (.139) [-.015]	-.082 (.142) [-.028]	-.104 (.154) [-.037]	.060 (.156) [.021]
Female	-.164 (.044) [-.058]	-.170 (.045) [-.060]	----	----	----	----
Black	.317 (.055) [.111]	.313 (.056) [.109]	.278 (.075) [.096]	.271 (.076) [.093]	.357 (.084) [.127]	.352 (.085) [.123]
Hispanic	.117 (.057) [.041]	.132 (.057) [.046]	.114 (.076) [.039]	.129 (.076) [.044]	.128 (.086) [.045]	.128 (.087) [.045]
Years of education	.003 (.011) [.001]	.006 (.012) [.002]	.031 (.016) [.011]	.031 (.016) [.011]	-.028 (.017) [-.010]	-.023 (.018) [-.008]
AFQT score	-.018 (.028) [-.006]	-.024 (.028) [-.008]	-.063 (.036) [-.022]	-.071 (.037) [-.025]	.031 (.044) [.011]	.024 (.044) [.008]

Table 9 continued

Experience (years)	.030	.031	.018	.020	.048	.049
	(.029)	(.029)	(.042)	(.042)	(.040)	(.040)
	[.011]	[.011]	[.006]	[.007]	[.017]	[.017]
Experience squared/10	-.013	-.014	-.006	-.007	-.023	-.024
	(.012)	(.012)	(.018)	(.018)	(.018)	(.018)
	[-.005]	[-.005]	[-.002]	[-.002]	[-.008]	[-.008]
Tenure (years)	-.109	-.108	-.125	-.123	-.099	-.094
	(.014)	(.014)	(.019)	(.019)	(.022)	(.022)
	[-.039]	[-.038]	[-.043]	[-.042]	[-.035]	[-.033]
Tenure squared/10	.048	.048	.055	.054	.045	.042
	(.009)	(.009)	(.012)	(.012)	(.014)	(.014)
	[.017]	[.017]	[.019]	[.019]	[.016]	[.015]
Promotion in last two years	.445	.434	.359	.351	.538	.527
	(.051)	(.051)	(.069)	(.069)	(.075)	(.076)
	[.155]	[.150]	[.123]	[.119]	[.189]	[.184]
On-site seminar or training program in last two years	.314	.313	.438	.448	.174	.163
	(.054)	(.054)	(.078)	(.078)	(.076)	(.077)
	[.109]	[.108]	[.146]	[.148]	[.062]	[.057]
Off-site seminar or training program in last two years	-.022	.008 [a]	-.007	-.010	-.028	.011
	(.079)	(.791)	(.118)	(.119)	(.107)	(.108)
	[-.008]	[.003]	[-.002]	[-.004]	[-.010]	[.004]
Private sector	.075	-.047	-.023	-.106	.145	.002
	(.059)	(.072)	(.087)	(.113)	(.085)	(.098)
	[.027]	[-.016]	[-.008]	[-.036]	[.052]	[.001]
Non-profit sector	-.081	-.087	-.189	-.185	-.009	-.018
	(.091)	(.091)	(.146)	(.146)	(.118)	(.119)
	[-.029]	[-.031]	[-.067]	[-.065]	[-.003]	[-.006]
Union status	.009	.029	.045	.062	.002	.015
	(.054)	(.054)	(.071)	(.072)	(.084)	(.085)
	[.003]	[.010]	[.016]	[.021]	[.001]	[.005]
Log of establishment size	.116	.119	.104	.099	.130	.140
	(.011)	(.011)	(.014)	(.015)	(.016)	(.017)
	[.041]	[.042]	[.036]	[.034]	[.046]	[.049]
Marital status	.057	.056	.135	.143	-.038	-.046
	(.046)	(.046)	(.069)	(.069)	(.064)	(.065)
	[.020]	[.020]	[.047]	[.050]	[-.014]	[-.016]
Number of children	-.053	-.052	-.072	-.073	-.062	-.057
	(.020)	(.020)	(.028)	(.028)	(.029)	(.030)
	[-.019]	[-.018]	[-.025]	[-.025]	[-.022]	[-.020]

Table 9 continued

Child aged 6 or less	.151	.152	.212	.207	.091	.101
	(.048)	(.049)	(.069)	(.070)	(.069)	(.070)
	[.053]	[.053]	[.073]	[.071]	[.032]	[.035]
Intercept	-.622	-.563	-.747	-.802	-.581	-.282
	(.236)	(.263)	(.339)	(.368)	(.348)	(.414)
Industry dummy vars.?	No	Yes	No	Yes	No	Yes
N	4,626	4,626	2,569	2,569	2,057	2,057
log likelihood	-2,873	-2,855	-1,566	-1,557	-1,283	-1,267

Note: Standard errors in ( )s, marginal effects in [ ]s. Also included in equations are indicators for urban location and South region.

[a] Coefficient, standard error, and marginal effect have been multiplied by 10.